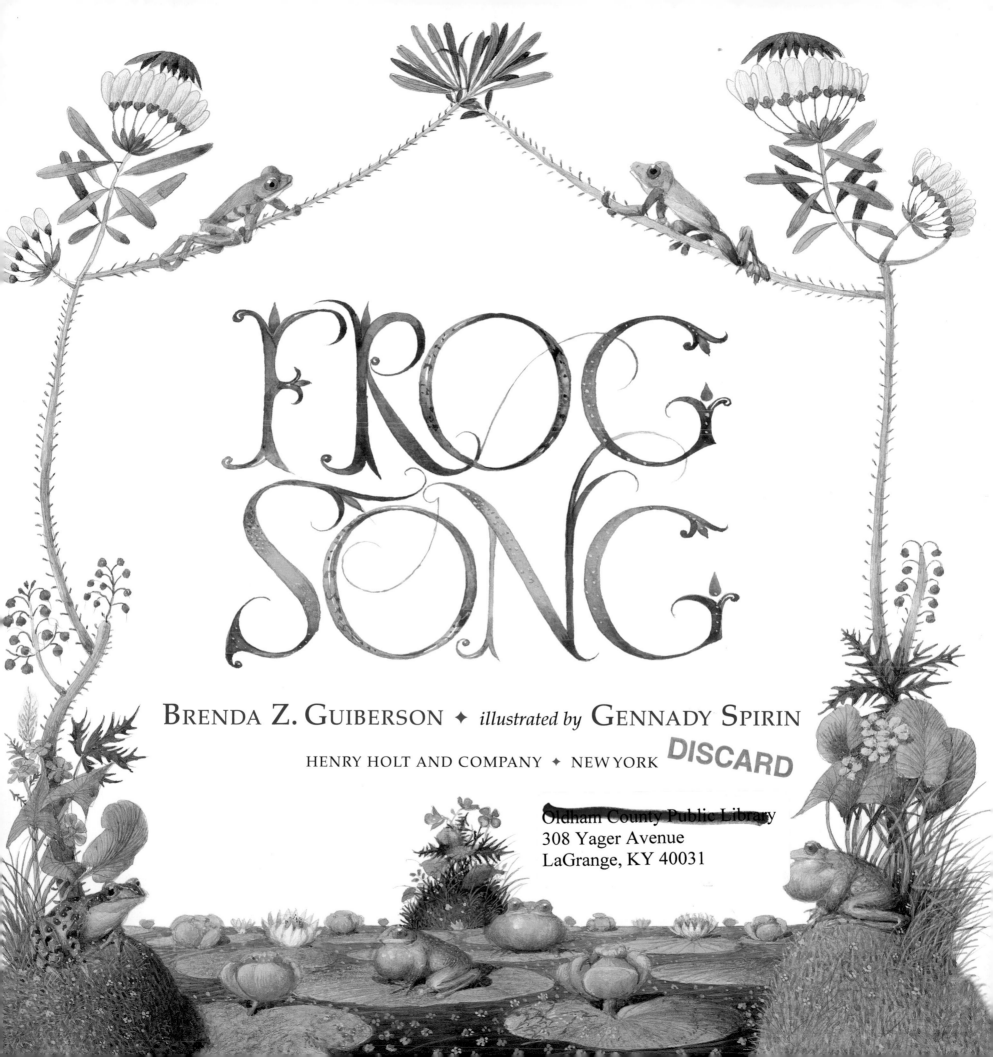

FROG SONG

BRENDA Z. GUIBERSON ✦ *illustrated by* GENNADY SPIRIN

HENRY HOLT AND COMPANY ✦ NEW YORK

*With thanks to Laura Godwin,
Noa Wheeler, Patrick Collins, and Kate Butler
for their inspired and creative work on this book.*

Henry Holt and Company, LLC
Publishers since 1866
175 Fifth Avenue
New York, New York 10010
mackids.com

Library of Congress Cataloging-in-Publication Data
Guiberson, Brenda Z.
Frog song / by Brenda Z. Guiberson ; illustrations by Gennady Spirin. — 1st ed.
p.   cm.
ISBN 978-0-8050-9254-7 (hc)
1. Frogs—Behavior—Juvenile literature. 2. Frogs—Vocalization—Juvenile literature.
I. Spirin, Gennady, ill. II. Title.
QL668.E2G853 2012   597.8′9—dc23   2011041940

First Edition—2012 / Designed by Patrick Collins
The artist used tempera, watercolor, and pencil on Arches watercolor paper to create the illustrations for this book.
Printed in China by South China Printing Co. Ltd., Dongguan City, Guangdong Province
1 3 5 7 9 10 8 6 4 2

To those working to restore frogs,
frog habitats, and wonderful frog songs
—B. Z. G.

To all those who love nature
—G. S.

Frogs have a song for trees, bogs, burrows, and logs. When frogs have enough moisture to keep gooey eggs, squirmy tadpoles, and hoppity adults from drying out, they can sing almost anywhere. CROAK! RIBBIT! BZZZT! PLONK!

BRACK!

THRUM-RUM!

In the rain forest of Costa Rica, the strawberry poison dart frog trills a tiny tune in a pile of wet leaves. PSSST-PSSST. The female hops over to lay five eggs. SQUISHY-SQUIRM! When the tadpoles hatch, she carries each of them to a separate pool of water high in the trees.

In Oklahoma, the Great Plains narrow-mouthed toad stays moist in a shady spider hole until it rains. Then he emerges to belt out a song. BUZZBUZZBUZZ! He lives with a tarantula and keeps the burrow free of insects. ZAP! The tarantula eats some frogs, but not this one.

In Ecuador, the song of the Surinam toad rattles across the swamp. **CLICK-CLACK**. The female carries 100 eggs in the skin on her back. A toad with no tongue, she dips and dives for food in the mud. **SLOOP-SLOOOP!** After four months, small froglets break through her skin and swim away.

In northeastern Australia, the Scarlet-sided pobblebonk sings by a pond after heavy rain. **BONK ... BONK ... BONK**. The female frog lays her eggs on the water and whips the gooey mass into a ball of bubbles. **FWISH!** This floating raft protects the eggs until the tadpoles hatch.

In Spain, the song of the male midwife toad clangs like a bell. **TINKTINKTINKTINK!** He carries a string of sticky eggs and crouches under a wet log to keep them moist. **SQUIZZLE-SQUIZ.** When he feels the tadpoles squirming, he hops, hops, hops to find a pool where they can hatch.

In Chile, the Darwin's frog sings in the beech forest. **CHIRP-CHWEET!** The male guards 30 eggs in the damp leaves for three weeks. When the tadpoles wiggle, he scoops them into his mouth. **SLURP!** They slither into his vocal sacs, where he keeps them safe and moist for seven weeks. Then he gives a big yawn, and little froglets pop out.

In Ethiopia, the shovel-nosed frog bellows a song from a dried-out pond. BUZZZZZZZZZ! The female uses her pointy snout to dig a burrow. She keeps her eggs moist until heavy rain floods the nest. DRIZZLE-DROP! The tadpoles hatch, and the nest starts to dry up. The mother digs a channel through the mud so the tadpoles can slide into a larger pool before they dry out.

In Borneo, the four-lined tree frog whistles a song. **SWEE-SWEE!** The female lays eggs on a leaf dangling over a stream. **SWIZZLE-SWISH!** She stirs up a foamy nest to keep the eggs moist. When the tadpoles break out, they plop into the water below.

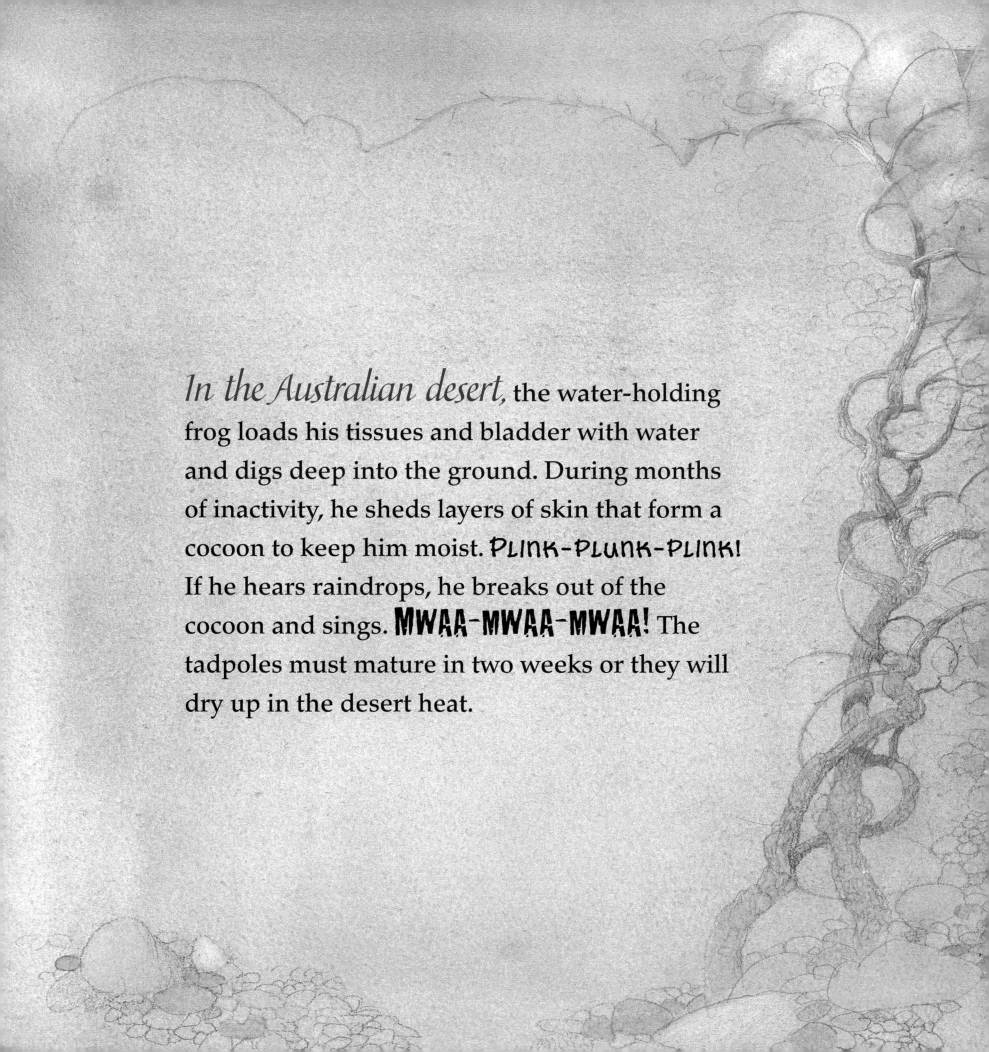

In the Australian desert, the water-holding frog loads his tissues and bladder with water and digs deep into the ground. During months of inactivity, he sheds layers of skin that form a cocoon to keep him moist. PLINK-PLUNK-PLINK! If he hears raindrops, he breaks out of the cocoon and sings. MWAA-MWAA-MWAA! The tadpoles must mature in two weeks or they will dry up in the desert heat.

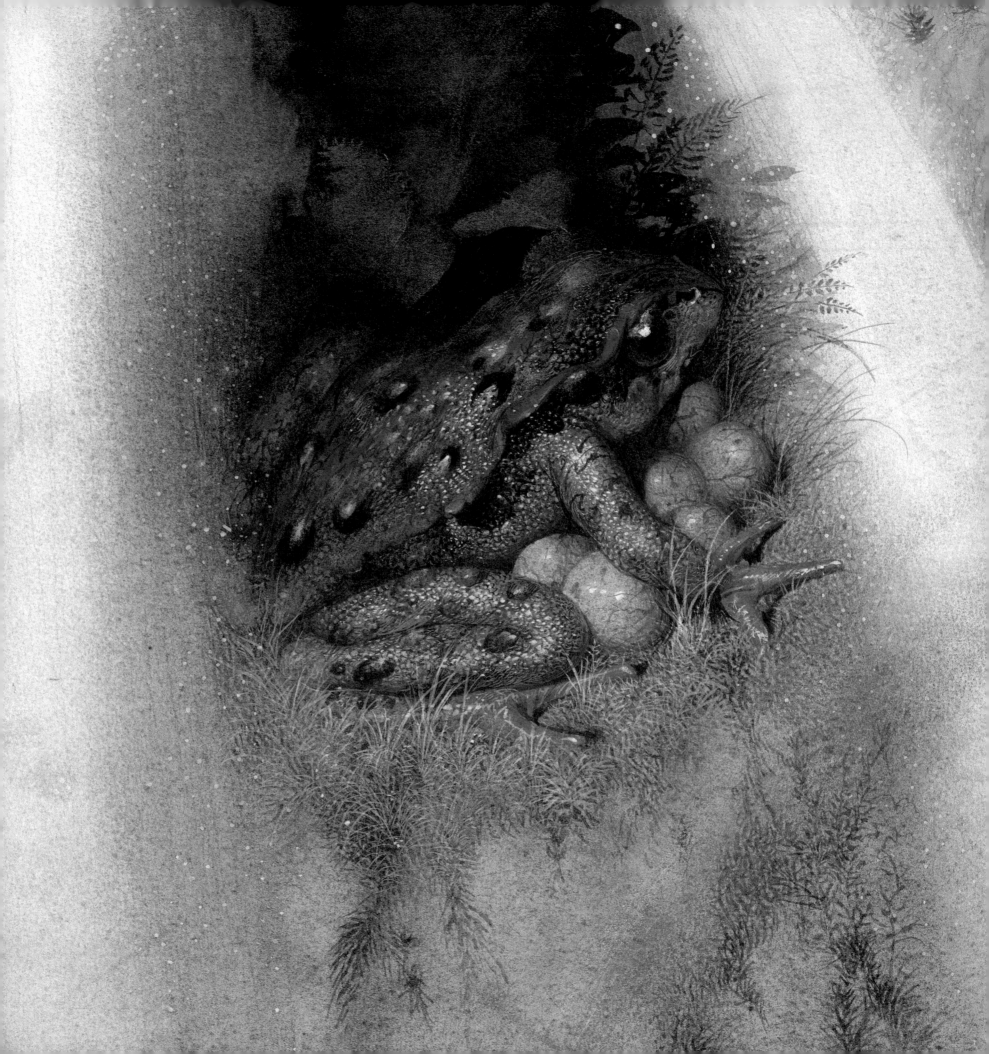

On a mountain ridge in New Zealand, the Archey's frog warbles in the mist of a waterfall. CHIRP CHIRP CHIRP! He sits on the egg mass to keep it moist. WRIGGLE-WRIGGLE! After five weeks, tiny froglets hop out.

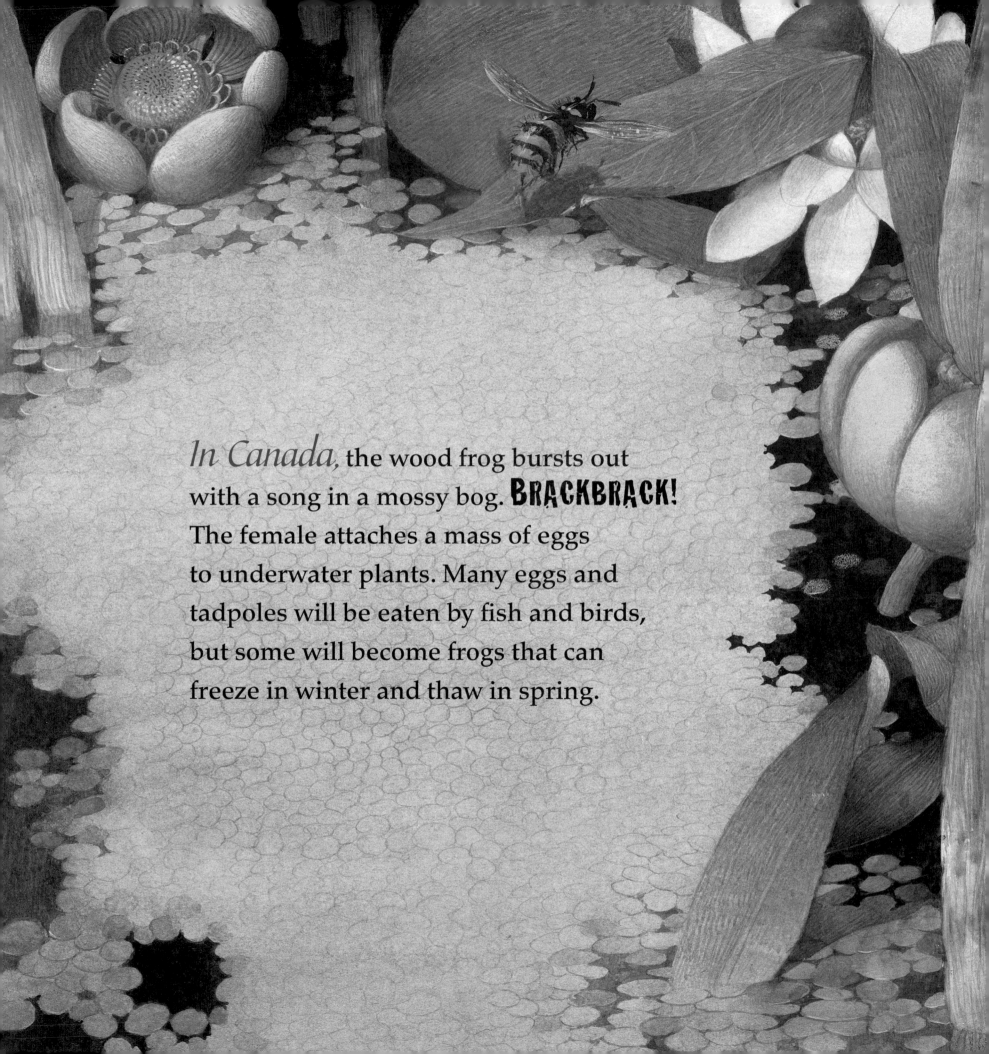

In Canada, the wood frog bursts out with a song in a mossy bog. **BRACKBRACK!** The female attaches a mass of eggs to underwater plants. Many eggs and tadpoles will be eaten by fish and birds, but some will become frogs that can freeze in winter and thaw in spring.

A frog song is a celebration of clean water, plants, and insects to eat. **CHIROOP, PRIBBLE!** Thousands of frog species have been singing and zapping since the time of the dinosaurs. Every day, in so many places, they add their ribbits and bellows to the music of the earth.

Frogs of the World

SURINAM TOAD

RANGE: Ecuador, Peru, Brazil, Venezuela, and the Guianas

LENGTH: Can reach 8 inches, but usually about 5 inches

QUICK FACT: This frog has no eyelids and no tongue, but lunges quickly to catch worms and small fish. It is the world's flattest frog.

SCARLET-SIDED POBBLEBONK

RANGE: Queensland and New South Wales in Australia

LENGTH: Almost 3 inches

QUICK FACT: Its hind legs have bright red markings on the inside that are revealed when the frog jumps. This red flash startles predators.

STRAWBERRY POISON DART FROG

RANGE: South America, from Nicaragua through Costa Rica and Panama

LENGTH: Very small, about one inch

QUICK FACT: This tiny frog travels between many rain forest plants to deposit extra eggs for her tadpoles to eat.

GREAT PLAINS NARROW-MOUTHED TOAD

RANGE: North America, from Nebraska through Texas and into Mexico

LENGTH: Can reach 1.5 inches

QUICK FACT: Its skin is very smooth and there is no webbing on the hind feet. With its small mouth it eats small insects like ants and termites.

MIDWIFE TOAD

RANGE: Portugal and Spain through France to Belgium, Netherlands, Luxembourg, Germany, and Switzerland

LENGTH: 1.5 inches

QUICK FACT: Its back is covered with poisonous warts that protect both the adults and the egg strings carried by the male. The tadpoles are giants, growing to over 4 inches long.

DARWIN'S FROG

RANGE: Chile and Argentina

LENGTH: About 1 inch

QUICK FACT: In response to danger, the frog rolls over and plays dead. Its belly looks like dead leaves. The tadpoles may absorb a fluid called "male's milk" that is produced in the father's vocal sacs.

SHOVEL-NOSED FROG

RANGE: Tropical and subtropical sub-Saharan Africa

LENGTH: Averages about 2 inches

QUICK FACT: Unlike other frogs that use hind limbs for digging, this frog's piglike snout is extremely hard and great for digging headfirst. The frog eats termites and ants. The tadpoles can be eaten by ants if not protected by the mother.

FOUR-LINED TREE FROG

RANGE: Northeast India, Bangladesh, Nepal, Borneo, Thailand, and Vietnam

LENGTH: Up to 2.5 inches

QUICK FACT: This frog is able to jump 7 feet. It has sticky pads on its toe tips to keep from slipping. It can climb walls and glass and survive in gardens and mud puddles. It also can change colors.

WATER-HOLDING FROG

RANGE: Spread across all states of Australia except Victoria and Tasmania

LENGTH: About 3 inches

QUICK FACT: It can store vast amounts of water in its tissues and extra-large bladder. In the dry season, Aborigines dig up this frog and gently squeeze out a drink. The frog can stay inactive in a burrow for years if needed.

ARCHEY'S FROG

RANGE: New Zealand

LENGTH: Can reach 1.5 inches

QUICK FACT: This frog has been around for 200 million years and is the smallest native frog on the islands of New Zealand. It has no tadpole stage. The males carry the froglets. These frogs use alternating hind legs to swim.

WOOD FROG

RANGE: From northern Georgia and northeastern Canada to Alaska and British Columbia

LENGTH: Averages about 2 inches

QUICK FACT: This frog can live north of the Arctic Circle and survives being frozen all winter. It comes out of hibernation before all the ice has melted along streams and is the first frog to deposit eggs.

Frogs in Trouble

Today, in a world crowded with humans, one third of our frogs are struggling to survive. What is making life so hard for frogs?

In many places, the water they need is dried up or polluted. *We need this water too. We drink it.*

Plants they use have been chopped down. *We need these plants too. They add oxygen to the air we breathe.*

The paths to ponds have been paved over and blocked. *We need these paths too as our walkways through nature.*

A fungus that kills frogs is thriving on our planet made warmer by human activity. *We need to understand how our behavior affects everything on earth.*

Every frog song is a wonder. A **MWAA-MWAA-MWAA** in the Australian desert is as delightful as a **TINKTINKTINK** in Spain. When a song is missing, the silence is a warning. Frogs can take care of themselves if we make sure they have what we all need—clear water, clean air, and plenty of plants.

Bibliography

ATTENBOROUGH, DAVID. *Life in Cold Blood*. Princeton, New Jersey: Princeton University Press, 2008.

BADGER, DAVID. *Frogs*. Stillwater, Minnesota: Voyageur Press, Inc., 1995.

BELTZ, ELLIN. *Frogs: Inside Their Remarkable World*. Buffalo, New York: Firefly Books, 2005.

BERNEY, CAROLE SMITH. "Big Night at the Vernal Pool." *Highlights for Children* (April 2008): 16–17.

BISHOP, NIC. *Frogs*. New York: Scholastic, 2008.

HAMILTON, GARRY. *Frog Rescue: Changing the Future for Endangered Wildlife*. Buffalo, New York: Firefly Books, 2004.

HOLLAND, JENNIFER S. "Vanishing Amphibians." *National Geographic* (April 2009): 138–53.

MATTISON, CHRIS. *300 Frogs: A Visual Reference to Frogs and Toads from Around the World*. Buffalo, New York: Firefly Books, 2007.

MILLER, SUSAN SWAN. *Amazing Amphibians*. New York: Franklin Watts, 2001.

MORGAN, SALLY. *Amphibians*. Chicago: Raintree, 2005.

PBS NATURE. *Frogs: The Thin Green Line*, DVD. 2009.

RAVVEN, WALLACE. "Biology on Ice." *Discover* (August 1994): 36–41.

TURNER, PAMELA S. *The Frog Scientist*. Boston: Houghton Mifflin Harcourt, 2009.

Frog Facts Online

http://allaboutfrogs.org/weird/general/songs.html

http://amphibiaweb.org/

http://www.aza.org/frogwatch/

http://animaldiversity.ummz.umich.edu/site/topics/frogCalls.html

http://www.bbc.co.uk/nature/life/Darwin's_Frog#intro

http://cgee.hamline.edu/frogs/

http://www.conservation.org/campaigns/lost_frogs/pages/frog_facts.aspx

http://www.enature.com/fieldguides/view_default
    .asp?curGroupID=7&shapeID=1056

http://www.exploratorium.edu/frogs/tracker/

http://www.frogsaustralia.net.au/frogs/display.cfm?frog_id=44

http://www.sciencedaily.com/releases/2004/10/041015103700.htm

http://www.waza.org/en/zoo/choose-a-species/amphibians/frogs-and-toads